Life Lab Science

How Things Work

Developed by Life Lab Science Program

Curriculum Director
Roberta Jaffe

ISBN 1–56307–204–1

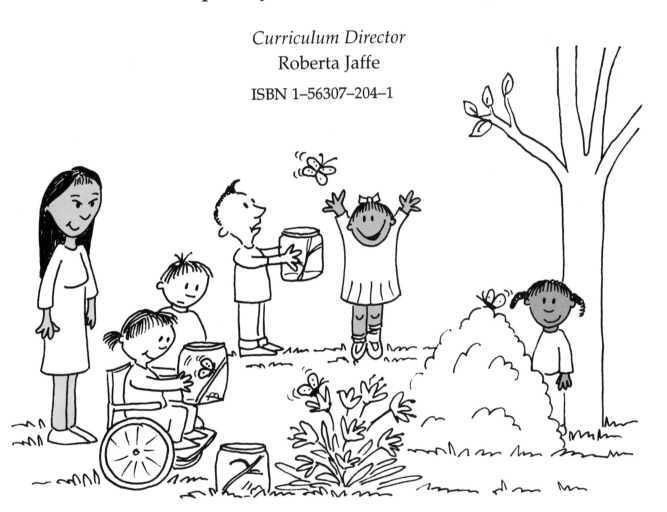

Table of Contents

Grade 3

Sensory Explorations

Month _____

Name _____

Monday	Tuesday	Wednesday	Thursday	Friday

Name_____Date_____

Which is the loudest: thunder, a rock concert, or a jet at take off?

Neither snakes nor fish have ears on their heads. How do they hear?

What my senses can tell me about the garden:

_____

_____

_____

_____

_____

Questions I have about the garden and what lives there:

_____

_____

_____

_____

_____

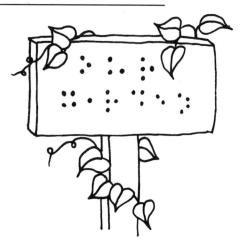

**What sense do people use to
read if they cannot see?**

**What senses are you using when
you eat?**

The Five Senses in the Garden, Part 2

Name_____Date_____

How did each sense help Nose answer the question?

Eye:_____

Hand:_____

Mouth:_____

Ear:_____

Write a new story. This time the sense with a question is Ear. Ear hears a scary sound in the garden. How do the other senses help? The story has been started for you. Finish it with a friend. Use extra paper if you need to. Be sure to give your story a title. Add pictures if you wish.

Title:_____

Ear walked into the garden. Alone. Just an ear. Suddenly, Ear heard a loud noise. "I wonder what that scary noise is," Ear said. Eye walked into the garden and looked around blinking. "Hello Ear," said Eye, shyly. "I am no good at hearing, but I can help you look for that scary noise."

_____

_____

_____

_____

_____

_____

_____

_____

My Mystery Object

Name_____Date_____

Look for an object in the garden that can be your mystery object. Draw a picture of it.

It smells:

_____

It looks:

_____

It sounds:

_____

It feels:

_____

Where I found it:

_____

It is a_____.

Observation Circles

Name_____Date_____

Study the plant very carefully. As you study it, take notes. The questions below will help you gather information.

What color or colors is it?_____

How does it smell?_____

How does it feel?_____

What shape are its leaves?_____

Are there any animals living on or around it?_____

_____

Has anything been eating it? If so, what damage do you see?

_____

Where is it growing?_____

Draw a picture of one part or detail of the plant.

What other questions can you ask about the plant?
List them below.

_____

_____

_____

_____

Garden Tools

Name_____Date_____

Name these tools! Explain how each is used. The first one is done
for you as an example.

Tool	Name	How Used
	Pitchfork	used for moving hay and making compost piles
	_____	_____ _____
	_____	_____ _____
	_____	_____ _____

Tool	Name	How Used

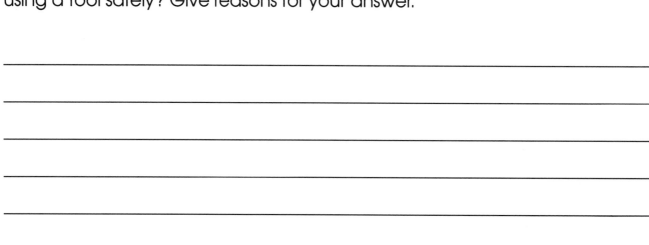

_____ _____

_____

_____ _____

_____

What would you do if you saw someone who was not using a tool safely? Give reasons for your answer.

_____

_____

_____

_____

_____

SAND
AND
OIL

Sensory Explorations
Postassessment

Name_____Date_____

Scientists measure sound in decibels. A watch
that is ticking measures 30 decibels. So does
a whisper. Thunder is about 100 decibels; a
rock concert is 120 decibels. A jet at take-off
measures 130 decibels. Noises louder than
130 decibels are painful.

Snakes have no ears, so they cannot
hear sounds through air. They pick up
low sounds from the ground. Fish hear
through their bodies.

What my senses told me about the garden:

_____

_____

_____

Questions I still have about the garden and what lives there:

_____

_____

_____

People use their sense of touch to read if they cannot see. Signs and books written in Braille have raised dots that stand for letters of the alphabet.

You use two senses when you eat: taste and smell. That is why nothing tastes good when your nose is stuffed up from a cold.

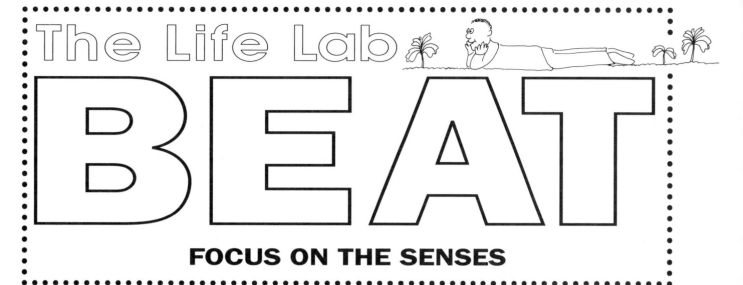

The Life Lab
BEAT

FOCUS ON THE SENSES

The Five Senses in the Garden

A Play

Characters:
NOSE

EYE

HAND

MOUTH

EAR

A CHORUS OF BEES

The Setting:
A beautiful garden with trees, bright-colored flowers, and plants with ripe fruit. EAR is sitting on a bench in the garden. MOUTH is standing in the shadow of a fruit tree.)

NOSE: (Walks into the garden,

alone.) "My, it smells good in here. I wonder what sweet-smelling thing lives in this garden." (NOSE walks around the garden, sniffing.)

EYE: (Walks into the garden. EYE looks around and blinks.) "Hello, Nose. I am not good at smelling. But I can help you look for this sweet-smelling thing. I see that lots of bright-colored flowers make their home in this garden. Maybe you are smelling this one with the pink petals."

(NOSE sniffs the flower.)

NOSE: "Oh, it does smell sweet! But that isn't it."

(HAND walks into the garden, reaches out and touches different things.)

HAND (shouting): "Ouch! Maybe you are smelling the roses that live in this corner. They have sharp thorns. But their flowers feel soft and silky."

NOSE (sniffing the air): "What a lovely smell! But no, that's not it either."

(A loud slurping noise is heard across the garden. There, in the shadows, is a giant MOUTH.)

MOUTH (smiling and chewing): "Sluurp! I am tasting a most delicious fruit. It is juicy and very sweet. Maybe it is what you smell?"

NOSE (sniffing the air): "Oh, that does smell good! But that's not it either."

EAR (listening quietly from the garden bench): "Maybe I can help you. I hear the sound of leaves blowing and falling. Maybe you smell the fallen leaves. I hear bees buzzing, too.

(CHORUS OF BEES makes a buzzing noise.)

EAR: "These bees make honey here. Perhaps you smell their sweet

honey here in the garden."

NOSE (sighs and sniffles): "No. That's not it."

(Suddenly NOSE jumps in the air and starts running around the garden, sniffing and sniffing. After a few circles, NOSE plops down on the ground. The others gather around.)

NOSE (shouting happily): "You were all right! You all helped me find part of the smell. This garden is home to many sweet-smelling things. There are flowers, fruit, leaves, and honey here. They all mix together into one wonderful smell. This whole garden is what smells so good!"

THE END

How Things Work

It's a Matter of Taste

When you bite into a cookie, you are using more than one sense. How can that be? Think about it. When you are eating a cookie you can see that it is a cookie. You can also smell it. You are not only using your sense of taste, but also your senses of sight and smell. If you don't believe it, try an experiment.

Ask a parent or a friend to cut up slices of peeled raw potato, apple,

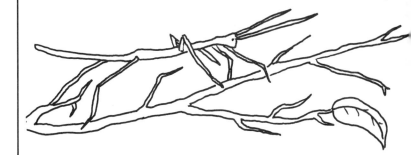

You have to look hard to see a walking stick. Guess how it got its name? Walking sticks are long, thin

and radish. Then hold your nose, close your eyes, and take a bite of each. Can you tell the radish from the potato? The apple from the radish? Probably not. Why? You do not have enough information to tell your brain what you are eating. When you eat, your brain gets information from your eyes and nose as well as your mouth.

Hidden in Plain View

Some animals have the same colors as their surroundings. They blend into the background. This is called *camouflage*. It helps them survive because it makes them difficult to see. Polar bears live in the arctic region where there is lots of snow. Because their fur is white, polar bears blend into the snowy landscape.

insects that look like twigs. They even have the same colors. They are brown and green or sometimes gray. They look so much like sticks that they are hard to spot until they move.

Some animals do not use color to hide. They show off their colors. The colors warn their enemies to stay away. One example is the monarch butterfly. It has a bad taste and can be poisonous. Its bright orange and black colors warn many birds that this butterfly would not be a tasty snack.

Did You Know?

- Crickets hear with their front legs.

- Lobsters taste with their feet.

- Fish hear through their bodies.

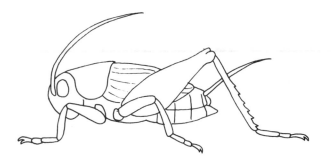

It's a Record!

Facts about the Senses

- Some people can tell the difference among as many as 300,000 different colors.

- The human ear can hear more than 1,500 different musical notes.

- Eagles have the best eyesight of all animals. An eagle can spot a hare from 3 kilometers away.

- A blue whale is the loudest animal. It can make sounds that can be heard 850 kilometers away.

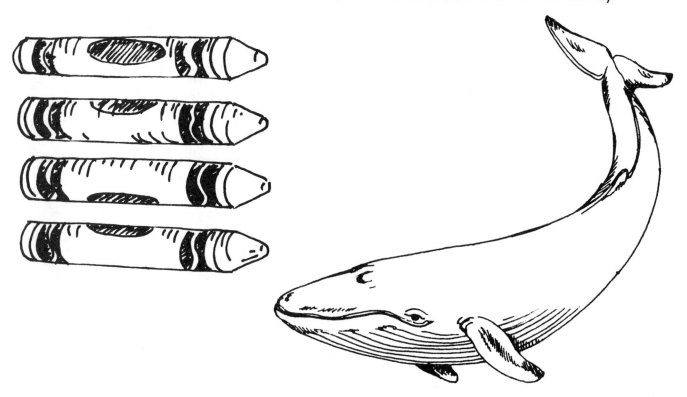

Seeds

Month

Monday	Tuesday	Wednesday	Thursday	Friday

Seeds
Preassessment

Name_____Date_____

What is the largest seed in the world?

Which is bigger: a poppyseed or a seed from a Giant Sequoia tree?

What I know about seeds:_____

_____

_____

_____

Questions I have about seeds:

_____

_____

_____

_____

How far can seeds travel in the air?

What do seeds have to do with velcro?

Seed Hunt

Name_____Date_____

Draw two of the seeds you found.

Name of seed:_____   Name of seed:_____

Where on the plant   Where on the plant
was the seed?   was the seed?

_____   _____

_____   _____

What do you think would have happened to the seeds
if you had left them on the plants?

_____

_____

More Adventures of the Seed Pod Pals

What do you think will happen to the Seed Pod Pals next?
Write the next chapter of their adventures in the space
below. Add new characters if you wish.

_____

_____

_____

_____

_____

_____

_____

_____

_____

_____

_____

_____

_____

_____

_____

_____

Seed Detectives

Name_____Date_____

Our Observations

Draw the parts of the seed you investigated.
Show all the parts. Give each part a name.

Our Ideas

Talk to other members of your group about your seed.
What do you think each part does? Let everyone
share ideas. Try to agree on one idea for each part.
Write the idea here:

1.   Name of part:_____

      What the part does:_____

2. Name of part:_____

What the part does:_____

3. Name of part:_____

What the part does:_____

4. Name of part:_____

What the part does:_____

Questions we have about the parts of a seed:

_____

_____

_____

_____

Shoots and Roots

Names_____Date_____

_____

Our Observations

Day 1	Day 2
Day 3	**Day 4**

GUESS

1. What do you think will happen to the seeds in the plastic bag in the next two days?

_____

_____

2. Why do you think this will happen?_____

_____

_____

TEST

Watch the seeds in the plastic bag. Draw a picture of them to show how they looked each time you checked them.

Day 5	Day 6

TELL

1. What did you learn by watching the seeds?

_____

_____

_____

2. Did the plant grow the way you thought it would?
Why or why not?

_____

_____

_____

Hitchhiker Seeds

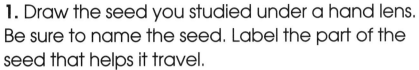

Name_____ Date_____

1. Draw the seed you studied under a hand lens. Be sure to name the seed. Label the part of the seed that helps it travel.

2. What would happen if all seeds dropped directly below the plant they grew on?

_____

_____

_____

3. What are two differences between seeds that stick
to the sock or blanket and seeds that don't stick?

_____

_____

_____

4. Look at the hitchhiker seed under a hand lens.
Draw what the sticky part looks like.

The Life of a Seed

Name_____Date_____

Write a story about the seed you planted. Include pictures.

Title:_____

Hanging Out on the Parent Plant

_____

_____

_____

_____

_____

_____

_____

Waiting for the Right Conditions

_____

_____

_____

_____

_____

_____

_____

_____

Becoming a Plant

_____

_____

_____

_____

_____

_____

_____

_____

_____

_____

_____

_____

Seeds Postassessment

Name_____Date_____

The "coconut of the sea" tree has seeds that can weigh over 23 kilograms (40 pounds) and yet can float hundreds of miles.

The Giant Sequoia tree can grow to 100 meters (300 feet) tall. But it starts as a tiny seeds that weighs 4 mg (1/6000th of an ounce).

What I learned about seeds:

_____

_____

_____

_____

Questions I still have about seeds:

_____

_____

_____

_____

_____

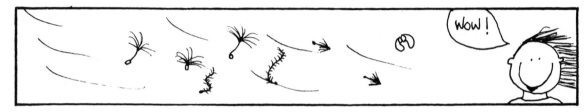

There are records of seeds traveling up to 50 kilometers (32 miles) on very strong winds.

The person who invented velcro got the idea from hitchhiker seeds.

The Adventures of the Seed Pod Pals

A Skit

Characters:
K. ABLE, TV ANNOUNCER

P. SEED

OTHER SEEDS

The Setting:
A school garden with trees and garden plants.

K. ABLE: "Welcome to WPOD news. We are reporting live from the garden. After waiting for weeks, it looks

like today may be the day for our big story. (Suddenly the wind blows and leaves start to fall. Seed pods begin to rattle.)

K. ABLE (in an excited voice): "This is the moment we have been waiting for!"

(At this moment the seeds arrive. They skid and jump into the garden. They come to a stop near K. ABLE.)

K. ABLE (excited, turns to one seed): "Excuse me! Can you tell our viewers your name?"

SEED: "Sure, my name is P. Seed."

K. ABLE: "P. Seed, can you tell us what brings you here?"

SEED: "As you know, seeds are very important. We contain baby plants that are covered by a seed coat. By the way, how do you like my coat?"

K. ABLE: "It's very nice. But can you tell us how you got here?"

SEED: "That's easy. My pals and I were inside a dry pod. We had to wait and wait until the conditions were right. Seeds are very good at waiting, you know."

K. ABLE: "Can you tell us about those conditions?"

SEED: "Sure. The wind needed to blow. It had to blow hard enough to rattle our pod and shake us loose. Our pod popped open and here we are."

K. ABLE: "Do all seeds arrive that way?"

SEED: "Oh no. My friend Dandy Lion gets to fly on the wind and parachute down. Another friend, Coco Nut, sometimes floats to a new home. Seeds can travel in lots of different ways."

K. ABLE: "That's amazing, P. Seed. What happens next?"

SEED: "My pals and I will stay right here and wait again. Why don't you check back with us later and see for yourself?"

K. ABLE: "Thank you, P. Seed. This is an exciting day in the garden. That's it for today. Please join us later for our next report."

(Months later. It is spring.)

K. ABLE: "Hello, this is K. ABLE from WPOD. We are joining the seed pod pals back in the garden. Last time we saw them, they had just arrived from their pod. Now let's see where their adventure has taken them."

(K. ABLE looks around.) "Hmm. I don't see them." (Pokes in the dead leaves.)

SEED: "Ouch!" (K. ABLE brushes away the dead leaves.) "Be careful!"

K. ABLE: "Hello. Maybe you can help me. I'm here to interview the seed pod pals. Have you seen them?"

SEED: "That's us! I guess you don't recognize us. We've had more adventures since you were last here!"

K. ABLE: "What happened?"

SEED: "It was amazing! First the fall leaves started to cover us. Then bits of soil. Before you knew it, we were covered up. Winter came. It was cold in the soil. Then it started to rain."

K. ABLE (excited): "What happened when you got wet?"

SEED: "My pals and I started to get bigger and bigger. We thought we would burst!"

K. ABLE (more excited than before): "Then what? Was it still cold?"

SEED: "Oh no. It was getting warmer. The sun must have been warming the soil. You know how nice it feels in the warm sun . . ."

K. ABLE (interrupts): "But tell us what happened next?"

SEED: "You remember my lovely seed coat? Well, I soaked up so much water that I split it! Then, roots began to grow. And I felt myself pushing my way out of the soil and here I am. A seedling! Watch it! My leaves are starting to uncurl. Who knows what will happen next!"

K. ABLE: "Who knows is right!" (Turns toward audience) "Thank you for joining us for this special report. Join us again for the next seed pod pals adventure!"

THE END

A Gripping Tale

Have you ever had a burr stick to your clothes after a walk outdoors? Did you rip it off and forget about it? That's what most people do. But not George de Mestral, an inventor from Switzerland. About 40 years ago he was pulling off the burrs that clung to his pants and socks, when he had an idea. He saw that each burr was a seed container covered by tiny hooks. The burrs had latched onto his clothing with these hooks.

De Mestral copied the idea and made a fastener. One half of the fastener was lined with tiny hooks like those on a burr. The other half held loops. You probably use that fastener every day. It is called *velcro*.

Seeds in Motion

Have you ever visited a meadow or even an open field on a breezy day in late summer or early fall? Did you notice floating seeds of thistle and milkweed plants? Dandelion seeds are floaters too. Drop one out a window and you will discover how it is like a parachute. Floaters often travel miles before they settle to the ground.

Try It!

Collect different kinds of seeds and see how each travels. Why do you think a seed has to travel?

It's a Record!

Largest seed is the coco-de-mer, a kind of palm tree. One seed can weigh as much as 23 kilograms (50 pounds).

Among the **smallest seeds** are daisy seeds. A million daisy seeds together weigh just one ounce.

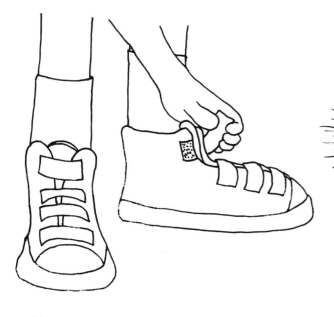

Soil

Name

Month

Monday	Tuesday	Wednesday	Thursday	Friday

Soil

Preassessment

Name_____Date_____

How many kinds of soil are there?

How is an earthworm like a plow?

What I know about soil:

_____

_____

_____

_____

_____

Questions I have about soil:

_____

_____

_____

_____

_____

How much of the Earth is covered by soil?

What do mountains, wind, and water have to do with soil?

Which Soil Do Plants Prefer?

Names_____Date_____

_____State_____

Investigation: In which state's soil do plants grow best?

GUESS (what we think will happen and why):

_____

_____

_____

_____

TEST (how we are going to find out):

1. _____

2. _____

3. _____

4. _____

5. _____

TELL (what we found out and what it means):

_____

_____

_____

_____

Which Soil Do Plants Prefer?

Test Results

Our State: _____ Seed Name: _____ Planted on: _____

After 1 week

After 2 weeks

After 3 weeks

After 4 weeks

Mudshakes

Names_____

_____

Date_____

State_____

What will happen when we mix our state soil with
water and then let it settle?

GUESS (what we think will happen and why):

_____

_____

_____

TEST (what we are doing to find out if our guess is right):

1._____

2._____

3._____

4._____

5._____

TELL (what we found out):

1._____

2._____

3._____

4._____

5._____

Mudshake
Test Results

Draw what your mudshake looks like.
Tape the strip with your mudshake layers
in the box next to the jar. In the jar write
words to describe each layer.

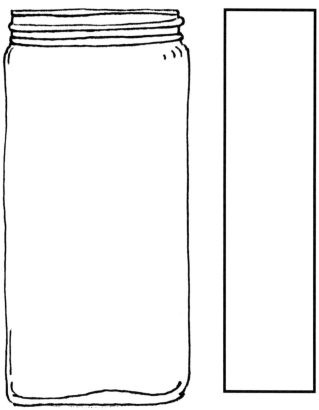

Do you think your soil is easy or hard

to dig in?_____

Why?_____

_____

Does your soil have more heavy, big pieces of sand or more small,

light pieces of clay?_____

How is your plant growing in this soil?_____

_____

Earthworms' Earth Stories

Part 1

Name_____Date_____

Write the next chapter in the Earthworm story. Suppose leaves and other matter did not break down. What would happen to the soil? To the earthworms? To the plants? To us?

_____

_____

_____

_____

_____

_____

_____

_____

_____

_____

_____

_____

_____

_____

_____

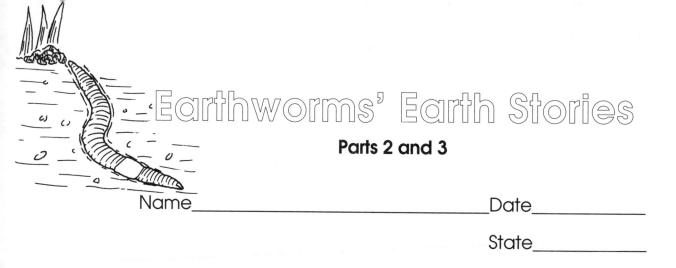

Earthworms' Earth Stories

Parts 2 and 3

Name_____Date_____

State_____

Investigation: What difference do you think the earthworms will make to your state soil?

GUESS (what we think will happen and why):

_____

_____

TEST (what we are doing to find out):
Draw a picture showing how your jar of test soil looks at the start of the experiment. Beside it draw a picture of the control.

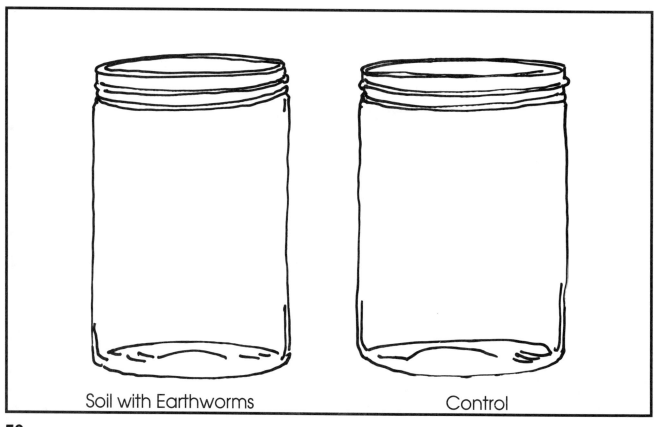

Soil with Earthworms   Control

TELL (what we found out and what it means):

_____

_____

_____

_____

Draw a picture showing how your test soil looked at the end of the experiment. Beside it draw a picture of the control.

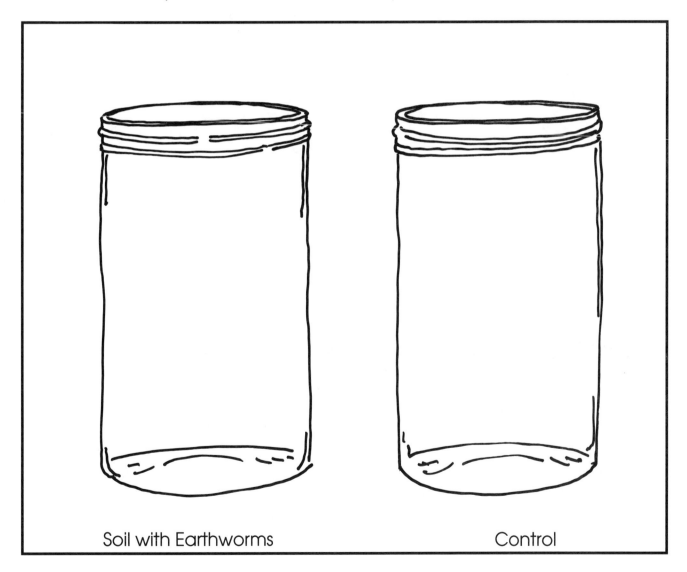

Soil with Earthworms   Control

Does It Hold Water?

Names_____Date_____

_____State_____

GUESS

Compare your state soil with the soils of other states.
Which will hold the most water? The least? How do
you think your soil ranks? Mark an X on the container
that represents your soil.

Holds the
most water

Holds some
water

Holds the
least water

TEST

How much water passed
through your soil? Mark the
amount on the measuring cup.

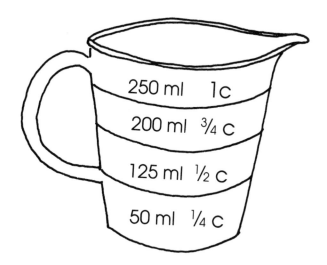

250 ml   1c

200 ml   ¾ C

125 ml   ½ C

50 ml   ¼ C

TELL

Show how well your soil holds water in comparison to the soil
of other states: Mark an X on the container that shows how
your state soil ranked.

Holds the
most water

Holds some
water

Holds the
least water

How does the amount of water your soil can hold affect plants growing in that soil? Give reasons for your answer.

_____

_____

_____

_____

_____

Soil

Postassessment

Name_____Date_____

Scientists divide soil into 11 groups. These groups include over 2,000 kinds of soil.

Both earthworms and plows break up the soil into fine pieces.

What I learned about soil:

_____

_____

_____

_____

_____

Questions I still have about soil:

_____

_____

_____

_____

_____

Only about 30 percent of the Earth is covered by soil. The rest is covered with water.

Wind and water make soil by wearing away rocks and stones. They can even wear away a mountain.

The Life Lab BEAT

FOCUS ON SOIL

The Dirt on Dirt

A Puppet Show

Characters:
Erin Earthworm

Dr. Wiggle Worm

The Setting:
Noisy Creek in the Great Gardener's garden, near an old, rotten log.

NEWS FLASH!!!! A special report from *TopSoil Times* reporter Erin Earthworm. Erin has an exclusive interview with a famous earth scientist, Dr. Wiggle Worm.

ERIN: "Thank you for joining us here at Noisy Creek, Dr. Wiggle Worm. Can you tell us how this soil got here? Where did it come from?"

DR. WORM: "Well, Erin, it all started a long, long time ago. Let's wiggle over here to these rocks. See these rocks along Noisy Creek? Long ago they were part of a much bigger rock up on that hill. (He points to the hill.)

Over thousands of years the heat and cold cracked the big rock. The rain beat down on it. The cracks got bigger and bigger. One day the rock finally broke into pieces. Those pieces of rock came tumbling down the hillside until they reached the side of the creek. Now those pieces of rock are slowly wearing away.

ERIN: Do rocks just wear away into

nothing? What happens to all the stuff that rocks are made of?

DR. WORM: That's a good question, Erin. The stuff that rocks are made of is called *matter*. Everything is made of matter. Now, as the rocks break down into tiny pieces, they become part of the soil. They become the little bits of sand, clay, and other minerals that make up the soil.

ERIN: Is that all soil is? Just worn-down bits of rock?

DR. WORM: That is one part of the soil, but there is another part, too. Soil also contains organic matter.

ERIN: *What* kind of matter?

DR. WORM: Organic matter is matter that was once alive. For example, this log was once a tall tree. It was struck by lightning one night and it fell to the ground. Now it slowly rots away. The leaves that fall from trees rot, too. So do bits of grass and fruit. They all become organic matter that is part of the soil.

ERIN: Does the organic matter just stay on top of the worn-down bits of rock?

DR. WORM: No, Erin, earthworms like you and me help turn rock and organic matter into rich soil. We recycle the organic material.

ERIN: How's that?

DR. WORM: As worms dig their tunnels, they move rocks around, and swallow bits of soil and organic matter. This material is ground up in a worm's gizzard and becomes a paste. Worms absorb from it the nutrients they need, and the leftovers become castings. These castings have nutrients that help plants grow. And worm tunnels let in air and water. All of this helps make a rich soil that's good for plants.

ERIN: Sounds like worms are great soil makers, Dr. Worm! Thank you for joining us. We hope you will come back again to answer more questions about soil. This is Erin Earthworm reporting for the *TopSoil Times*.

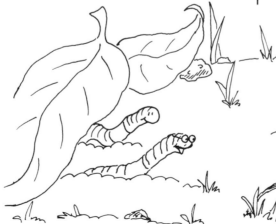

Soil in the Making

Every day, water and wind help turn rocks into soil. Look in your neighborhood for signs of how each wears away rocks. The effects of water are easier to spot.

• Look for what ice does to rocks. When water gets into a crack in a rock and turns to ice, it expands. So the crack gets even bigger.

• Look under rain gutters. Notice how falling water changes the ground near a rain gutter.

• Look for gullies. When water runs down a hill, it washes away soil and leaves behind small gullies. In time, a small gully can become a big one.

Why are smooth stones a sign of water at work? What about a pile of gravel on a sidewalk after a heavy rain? Make a list of all the ways water is working to create new soil in your neighborhood.

Is the Yellow Sea Really Yellow?

The Yellow Sea is in China. It gets its name from the yellowish soil that has washed into the sea over the years. The soil makes the water look yellow. China is not the only place where soil is being washed into the sea. It happens everywhere on earth.

Experts say that in the last 400 years, over $\frac{1}{4}$ of all the topsoil in the United States has been washed into the sea. How do people keep soil from washing away? One way is by planting trees. Tree roots hold the soil in place.

Did You Know?

• In nature it can take 500 years to form one inch of top soil.

It's a Record!

• An earthworm called the nightcrawler builds burrows that often go down one meter deep, and sometimes 2.5 meters deep.

MAKE A WORM PUPPET

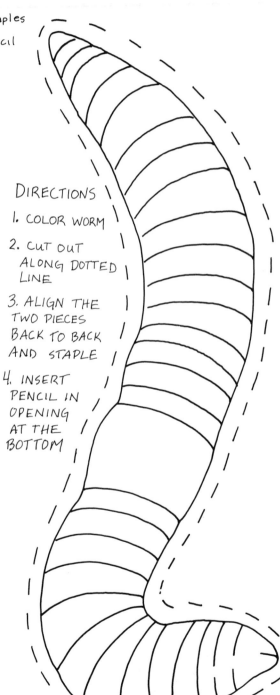

staples
pencil

DIRECTIONS

1. COLOR WORM

2. CUT OUT ALONG DOTTED LINE

3. ALIGN THE TWO PIECES BACK TO BACK AND STAPLE

4. INSERT PENCIL IN OPENING AT THE BOTTOM

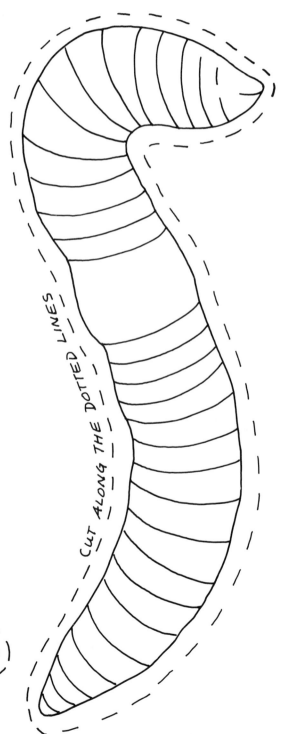

CUT ALONG THE DOTTED LINES

Weather and Climate

Name _____

Month _____

Monday	Tuesday	Wednesday	Thursday	Friday

Weather and Climate
Preassessment

Name_____Date_____

What was the highest temperature ever recorded? Where did it get that hot?

Burrr!

What was the lowest temperature ever recorded? Where did it get that cold?

What I know about weather:

_____

_____

_____

_____

_____

_____

Questions I have about weather:

_____

_____

_____

_____

_____

_____

How do cities affect the weather?

What is inside a thundercloud?

What's the Weather?

Name_____Date_____

Part 1. *And now for today's weather . . .*

1. What is the weather like today?

_____

_____

_____

2. How is the weather affecting plants, animals, and people?

_____

_____

_____

3. Is this weather typical for this season of the year?
Why or why not?

_____

_____

_____

4. How is the weather similar to the weather at other seasons
of the year? How is it different?

_____

_____

_____

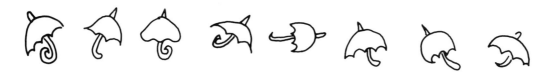

Part 2. *And now the forecast for tomorrow's weather . . .*

1. What will tomorrow's weather be like? Make a prediction.

_____

_____

_____

2. How will tomorrow's weather be like today's weather? Why do you think so?

_____

_____

_____

3. How will tomorrow's weather be different from today's weather? Why do you think so?

_____

_____

_____

4. How do you think tomorrow's weather will affect plants, animals, and people? Why?

_____

_____

_____

Thermometer Station

Name_____Date_____

How Warm Is It?

Thermometers measure temperature. They tell us how
hot or cold it is. There are two scales on the thermometer.
One measures temperatures in Fahrenheit. It is used in the
United States. The other measures temperatures in Celsius.
It is used in most other countries. The two scales are very
different. When it is 0 degrees on a Celsius scale, it is 32
degrees Fahrenheit.

Handy Things to Know about Thermometers:

• Thermometers break! Handle them carefully.

• Be patient while the thermometer measures
change—give it time.

• Do not touch the bottom tip of the thermometer when
measuring air temperature. If you do, it will measure the
temperature of your finger instead of the air.

• Do not hold a thermometer in direct sunlight when you
measure outside air. And, of course, don't put it down on
a hot or cold surface. (Can you figure out why?)

At the Thermometer Station:

Use the thermometers to measure the temperature in each of the places described below. Then color in the picture of the thermometer to show the temperature. Write the temperature in the spaces provided.

1. Show the indoor air temperature in Fahrenheit and Celsius.

_____ °

2. Show the temperature of the ice water in Fahrenheit and Celsius.

_____ °

3. Show the temperature of the hot water in Fahrenheit and Celsius.

_____ °

4. Show the temperature of the jar of water in Fahrenheit and Celsius.

_____ °

Tools for Watching Weather
Rain Gauge Station

Name_____Date_____

How Rainy Is It?
A rain gauge measures how much rain fell during a storm. It measures rain in inches or centimeters. An inch is a standard measurement, used mainly in the United States. A centimeter is a metric measurement, used in most other countries. There are about $2\frac{1}{2}$ centimeters in an inch.

Handy Things to Know about Rain Gauges:
• Place your empty gauge in an open place where rainfall will not be blocked by trees or overhanging buildings.

• Be sure the gauge is steady and in a place where it can't be knocked over.

• Be sure that the end of the ruler is touching the bottom of the gauge when you are reading the gauge.

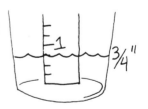

• After you take your measurement, dump the water out of the gauge so that you'll be ready for the next rainfall.

At the Rain Gauge Station:

Draw a line to show how much water is in each can. Then write the amount in inches.

1. Show how much water is in can #1 in inches.

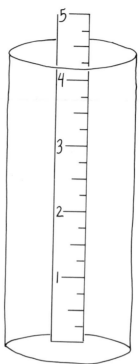

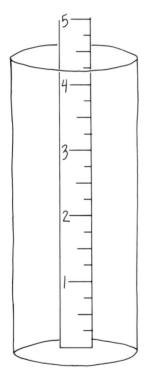

2. Show how much water is in can #2 in inches.

3. Show how much water is in can #3 in inches.

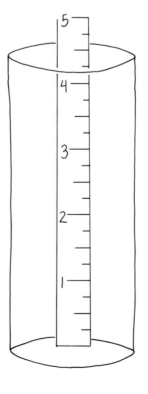

Windsock Station

Name_____Date_____

How Windy Is It?

A windsock can help you figure
out in what direction the wind is
blowing. It can also help you tell
how fast the wind is moving.

Handy Things to Know about Windsocks:

• Mount your windsock on a tall stick so that it can fly
freely in any direction.

• Be sure it is in a place where where it can't be
knocked over.

• Figure out where north, south, east, and west are. One
way to do so is to look for the sun. It is in the east in the
morning and the west in afternoon. If you are facing east,
north is to your left and south is to your right, where is west?

• Use the scale below to measure the wind:

At the Windsock Station:

Look at the way the windsock is held. Then circle the picture that looks most like your windsock. Circle the word that best describes the windspeed. Look at your school flag. Circle the picture that most looks like your windsock. Circle the word that best describes the windspeed.

No wind

Gentle breeze

Tingle Tingle Tingle

strong wind

Gusty wind

Instructions for Recording the Weather

1. Under the heading **Temperature,** use a red crayon or marker to color in the thermometer to match the temperature at your weather station.

2. Under the heading **Rain/Snow,** mark the amount of snow or rain on the ruler. Write how much it is in inches or centimeters in the space underneath.

3. Cut out the picture of the windsock that is at the same angle as your windsock. Tape it to the chart under the heading **Wind.**

4. Cut out the picture of the sky that best matches what the sky looks like today. Tape it to the chart under the heading **Sky.**

5. Under **Notes,** write about the water in the bucket. (Does it have a thin layer of ice on top? Is it frozen solid?) Tell, too, how the weather is affecting plants and animals in the garden.

Weather Watcher's Diary

Name _____   Date _____

Weather during the Week of _____

	Temperature	Rain/Snow	Sky	Wind	Notes
Monday					
Guess					
Test					
Tuesday					
Guess					
Test					
Wednesday					
Guess					
Test					
Thursday					
Guess					
Test					
Friday					
Guess					
Test					

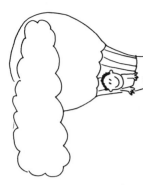

Weather Watcher's Diary

Name _____   Date _____

Weather during the Week of _____

		Temperature	Rain/Snow	Sky	Wind	Notes
Monday	Guess					
	Test					
Tuesday	Guess					
	Test					
Wednesday	Guess					
	Test					
Thursday	Guess					
	Test					
Friday	Guess					
	Test					

Weather Watcher's Diary

Name _____

Date _____

Weather during the Week of _____

		Temperature	Rain/Snow	Sky	Wind	Notes
Monday	Guess					
	Test					
Tuesday	Guess					
	Test					
Wednesday	Guess					
	Test					
Thursday	Guess					
	Test					
Friday	Guess					
	Test					

Weather Watcher's Diary

Name _____

Date _____

Weather during the Week of _____

	Temperature	Rain/Snow	Sky	Wind	Notes
Monday					
Guess					
Test					
Tuesday					
Guess					
Test					
Wednesday					
Guess					
Test					
Thursday					
Guess					
Test					
Friday					
Guess					
Test					

Weather Watcher Questions

Name_____Date_____

Temperature

1. What was the coldest temperature?

For the week of: _____

For the month:_____

2. What was the hottest temperature?

For the week of: _____

For the month:_____

3. How many days was it above freezing?

For the week of: _____

For the month:_____

4. How many days did the water in the frost bucket freeze?

For the week of: _____

For the month:_____

5. What observations were made about the plants and animals on the coldest and hottest days?

For the week of: _____

For the month:_____

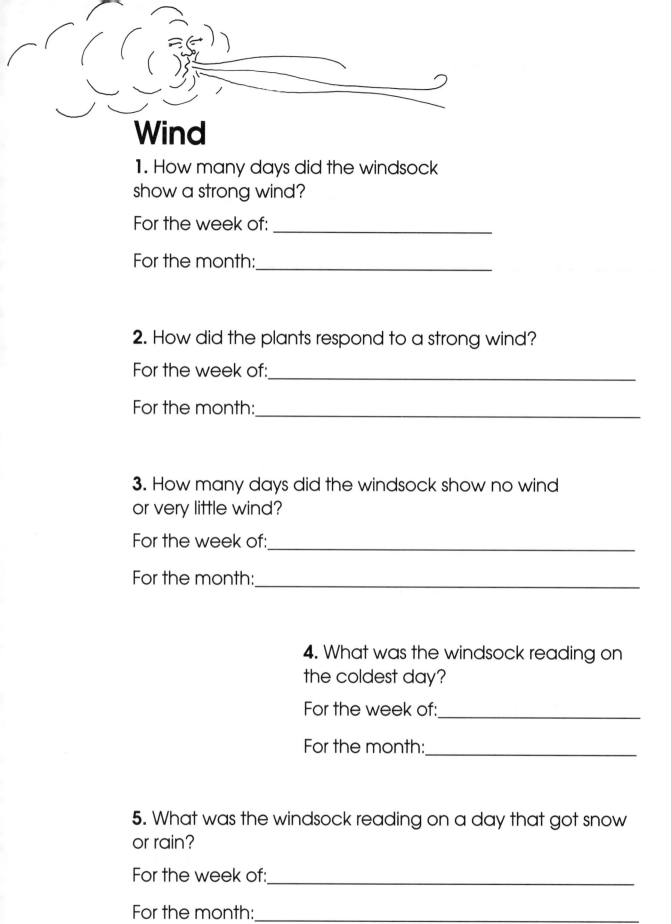

Wind

1. How many days did the windsock show a strong wind?

For the week of: _____

For the month:_____

2. How did the plants respond to a strong wind?

For the week of:_____

For the month:_____

3. How many days did the windsock show no wind or very little wind?

For the week of:_____

For the month:_____

4. What was the windsock reading on the coldest day?

For the week of:_____

For the month:_____

5. What was the windsock reading on a day that got snow or rain?

For the week of:_____

For the month:_____

Clear, Partly Cloudy, or Overcast?

1. How many days was the sky clear?

For the week of:_____

For the month: _____

2. How many days was the sky overcast?

For the week of:_____

For the month:_____

3. Were clear days warmer or colder than overcast days?

For the week of:_____

For the month:_____

4. Did it rain or snow on the days that were overcast?

For the week of:_____

For the month:_____

How many days did it rain or snow?

1. How many total inches or centimeters of rain or snow fell?

For the week of:_____

For the month:_____

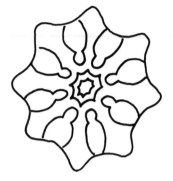

2. What was the most rain or snow in a day?

For the week of: _____

For the month:_____

3. What was the temperature on that day?

For the week of: _____

For the month:_____

4. What was the wind like on that day?

For the week of: _____

For the month:_____

5. How did the plants respond to the rain or snow?

For the week of:_____

For the month:_____

I Remember When . . .

Date _____

Interviewer_____

Interviewee_____

1. Where else in the country have you lived?

_____

2. How long did you live there?

_____

3. What's the worst weather that you remember there?

_____

4. What were the summers like there?

_____

5. What were the winters like there?

_____

6. How did the weather affect the soil, plants, and animals?

_____

7. Where else in the country or world have you lived?

_____

8. What were the summers like?

_____

9. What were the winters like?

_____

10. How did the weather there affect the plants and animals?

_____

Under the Weather

Name_____Date_____

Our question:_____
_____

GUESS: (how will the plant respond in one week?)

_____

_____

_____

_____

TEST: (what is your test plan?)

_____

_____

_____

_____

TELL: (what happened?)

_____

_____

_____

_____

A picture of our plant the day we started the test.

A picture of our plant one week late.

What do you think would happen if you continued this weather treatment for a month? Why?

_____

_____

_____

_____

Vegetable Planting Guide

Vegetable	Can It Take Frost?	Growing Range °C (°F)	Best Growing Temperature °C (°F)	Number of Weeks till Harvest (from seed)	When to Plant in Our Area	When to Harvest in Our Area	Should We Plant This in Our Class Garden?
Beans, bush	no	18–29 (65–85)	24 (75)	8			
Beans, pole	no	18–29 (65–85)	24 (75)	8–9			
Beets	some	7–27 (45–80)	18 (65)	8–9			
Broccoli	yes	7–27 (45–80)	21 (70)	8–9			
Brussels sprouts	yes	7–27 (45–80)	18 (65)	11–13			
Cabbage	yes	7–27 (45–80)	18 (65)	9–16			
Carrots	some	13–29 (55–85)	24 (75)	9–11			
Cauliflower	yes	7–27 (45–80)	18 (65)	8–12			
Celery	some	13–29 (55–85)	24 (75)	15–16			
Chard	some	7–29 (45–85)	21 (70)	7–8			
Corn	no	13–32 (55–90)	27 (80)	9–13			
Cucumber	no	18–35 (65–95)	27 (80)	7–10			
Eggplant	no	21–35 (70–95)	29 (85)	10–11			
Garlic	yes	7–27 (45–80)	16 (60)	17–26			
Kale	yes	7–27 (45–80)	18 (65)	8–9			
Kohlrabi	yes	7–27 (45–80)	18 (65)	7–8			
Leeks	yes	7–27 (45–80)	21 (70)	19			
Lettuce, leaf	some	10–29 (50–85)	21 (70)	6–13			
Melons	no	18–35 (65–95)	27 (80)	20			
Onion (from seed)	some	10–29 (50–85)	21 (70)	12–17			

Vegetable Planting Guide

Vegetable	Can It Take Frost?	Growing Range °C (°F)	Best Growing Temperature °C (°F)	Number of Weeks till Harvest (from seed)	When to Plant in Our Area	When to Harvest in Our Area	Should We Plant This in Our Class Garden?
Onion (from sets)	some	10–29 (50–85)	21 (70)	12			
Parsley	some	13–29 (55–85)	24 (75)	10–13			
Peas, pole	some	7–27 (45–80)	18 (65)	10-11			
Peppers	no	18–32 (65–90)	27 (80)	9–12			
Potatoes	no	7–29 (45–85)	18 (65)	17			
Pumpkin	no	13–32 (55–90)	24 (75)	14–16			
Radish	yes	7–27 (45–80)	18 (65)	3–9			
Spinach	some	7–27 (45–80)	21 (70)	6–7			
Squash, summer	no	13–32 (55–90)	24 (75)	6–10			
Squash, winter	no	13–32 (55–90)	24 (75)	11–17			
Sweet potato	no	18–35 (65–95)	27 (80)	26–34			
Tomatoes	no	13–29 (55–85)	24 (75)	8–13			
Turnips	yes	7–27 (45–80)	18 (65)	5–10			

Postassessment

Name_____Date_____

The highest temperature ever recorded was 136.4 degrees F at Al' Aziziyah, Libya, on September 22, 1922. It was almost that hot in Death Valley, California, on July 10, 1913. The temperature was 134 degrees.

The lowest temperature ever recorded was in Antarctica. On August 24, 1960, it was 126.9 degrees below zero F. The coldest temperature ever recorded in the United States was in Alaska. It was 80 degrees below zero F on January 23, 1971.

Burrr!

What I learned about weather:

_____

_____

_____

_____

Questions I still have about weather:

_____

_____

_____

_____

Cities are usually warmer than the suburbs because heat is trapped in narrow streets between tall buildings. Also, cars give off heat and gases that hang over the city like a blanket.

A thundercloud is made up of water. It may be snow, rain, sleet, or even hail.

The Life Lab BEAT

FOCUS ON WEATHER AND CLIMATE

History of a Desert Family

History. That means something that happened a long, long time ago, right? Not always. What happened yesterday is history, too!

Your Life Lab Journal is history. You are writing about things that happened. Your journal might include the history of a plant from the time you planted the seed until the plant produced its own seeds.

What else has a history? Your skateboard? Your family? Your school? Absolutely. How can you find out about the history of something? You can ask questions and write down everything you find out.

Here's what one Life Lab scientist did. Her name is Ann. Ann traveled to the hot, dry desert to visit her grandparents and to learn about farming in the desert. Ann's grandparents are Tohono O'odham, a native people in the Southwest.

A Trip to the Desert

My grandparents live in the Sonoran Desert in Arizona. The desert is a dry land, where months pass without a sign of rain.

Although it is winter, it is very warm outside. I follow Grandfather as he does his chores. As he works, Grandfather stops from time to time and studies the sky, watching for rain.

"Grandfather, what is it like here in summer?"

"Very hot," he says. "And very dry."

"How can you farm in a land with very little rain?"

"Our people have been farming in the desert for a very long time," said Grandfather. "Some people think it is impossible to grow crops in such a dry place. Even in good years the clouds bring only eight to twelve inches of rain a year. In bad years, there may be only three inches of rain."

"But grandfather, how can plants grow in a place that gets so little rain?"

"We have a special way of farming called akchin. In our language, akchin means "mouth of the arroyo." The arroyo is a dry river bed that fills with water only during a rainstorm. We plant our crops at the place where the water washes out from the arroyo onto flatter land.

"As soon as the rains come we quickly plant beans, corn, and squash seeds deep in the soil where they will stay moist. We plant our seeds far apart, so that one plant does not take water from another. After all, the rains may not come again for a long time. Our crops must grow quickly before the hot sun dries the land once again."

Grandfather laughed softly. He turned to me and asked, "What is it like to live in a land with lots of rain? Do you long for the sun? What kinds of plants do you grow where you live? Does cactus grow there? Tell me about your home."

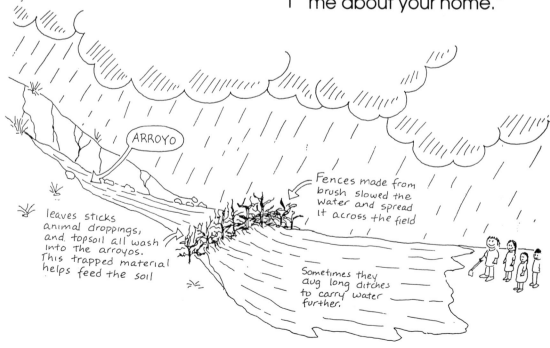

ARROYO

leaves sticks animal droppings, and topsoil all wash into the arroyos. This trapped material helps feed the soil

Fences made from brush slowed the water and spread it across the field

Sometimes they dug long ditches to carry water further.

Scientists at Work

Making the Desert Bloom

Israel's desert is thousands of miles from the ones in Arizona and New Mexico. Yet there, too, rain rarely soaks into the hard desert soil. There, too, rain washes away loose soil.

About 50 years ago, Michael Evenari, a professor at Hebrew University, found the remains of a group of ancient farmers. He wondered how they grew crops in such a dry place. He decided to find out. He rebuilt the ditches they had carved into rocky hillsides and their step-like fields.

It rained shortly after Evenari finished his work. For 30 minutes, it poured. Normally such a rain would cause flooding. It would also wash away soil from the hillsides. This time, however, the rain water and the loose soil ran into the stone ditches. The ditches carried the water and the soil to the fields Evenari rebuilt. There the water collected, and, in time, soaked into the ground. The scientist now had wet, rich soil for farming.

Evenari planted wheat, barley, and other crops. He also planted nut and olive trees. They grew year after year—even though some years the desert got less than five inches of rain. Today people come from all over the world to Israel to study how farmers over 1500 years ago grew crops in the desert.

How Things Work

Hail to Hail!

Sometimes raindrops are picked up by strong winds. They are flung high up in the air. Here the air is cold enough to freeze them into drops of ice. As they fall back toward the ground, more water condenses around each ice drop. They are then blown up again and a new layer of ice freezes around the old one. As they fall back to earth, they may be blown upward again and again. Each time the drops pick up another layer of ice. Finally, when they are too heavy for the wind to carry, they fall to the ground as hail.

Test It!

The next time it hails, collect a few hailstones. Ask an adult to help you cut one open. Inside you will see rings just as you do in an onion. Count the rings and you will know how many trips the hailstone made before it fell to earth.

A Human Hailstone

Did you know there was once a human hailstone? In 1930, some

German pilots were trying to see who could fly the highest. By accident they flew into storm clouds. Powerful winds carried them up higher and higher. Before they realized it, they were in trouble! Most of the pilots were able to safely bail out of their planes. But one pilot was picked up by the wind and flung into a cloud of super-cold water vapor. There he became the center of a huge hailstone. Layers of ice froze on him. As he fell, he unfroze and his parachute opened. Even he was amazed that he lived to tell the story!

Did You Know?

• There are 10 kinds of clouds. Each kind has a different shape.

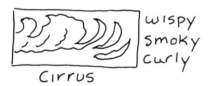
Cirrus — Wispy Smoky Curly

Stratus — Sheet cover flat, dull grey

Cumulus — Puffy, white cottony fluffy

• "The Windy City" is a nickname for Chicago, Illinois. But Chicago is not the windiest city in the United States. Great Falls, Montana; Oklahoma City, Oklahoma; Boston, Massachusetts; and Cheyenne, Wyoming, are all windier!

Folklore

Frogs Croak the Weather!

Many Chinese farmers don't bother to listen to the TV weather forecast. They just listen to the frogs croak. The farmers say that if frogs croak on a fair day, it will rain in two days. But if the frogs croak after it rains, there will be fair weather.

In Europe, many farmers also listen to the frogs. In Central Europe, someone invented a frog barometer. A tree frog and a tiny ladder are placed in a glass jar half-filled with water. If the frog stays in the water and croaks, the weather will be bad. If the frog climbs the ladder, the weather will be fair. If the frog stays on the top rung of the ladder, the weather will stay fair.

Does it work? Find a frog and see for yourself!

Tools

Name

Month

Monday	Tuesday	Wednesday	Thursday	Friday

Preassessment

Name_____Date_____

What animal has feathers, makes a hammering sound, and uses a tool? What tool does it use?

What I know about tools and work:

_____

_____

_____

_____

This animal tool-user lives in the ocean. When it eats it uses its chest as a tray. What is it? What tool

does it use?

Questions I have about tools and work:

_____

_____

_____

_____

This animal tool-user lives in Africa. It uses different kinds of tools. One kind of tool helps this animal catch food— termites! What's this animal's name? What kind of tool does it use?

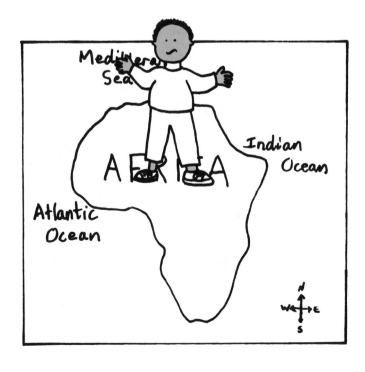

Seesaw Ups and Downs

Experimenters:_____Date_____

_____

I. Ruler Balance

1. Lay a ruler across an eraser to make a seesaw. The ruler is the seesaw board. The eraser is the fulcrum.

2. Put the cup on the ruler so that it balances with the cup that is taped to the ruler. **Draw** a picture of where you put your cup to make the ruler balance.

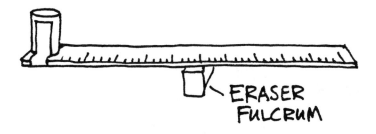

ERASER FULCRUM

3. Put 10 pennies or beans in the taped-on cup. How many pennies or beans must you put in your cup to balance the ruler?

GUESS_____

TEST your Guess.

TELL_____

_____

4. What happens if you put another penny in your cup?

_____

_____

Seesaw Ups and Downs

II. Seesaw

1. Empty the taped-on cup. Put the other cup on the 10 cm (4-inch) mark on the ruler. Put 10 pennies in your cup.

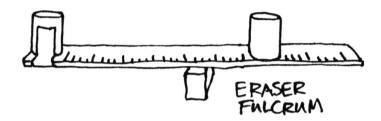

ERASER
FULCRUM

2. How many pennies must you put in the taped-on cup to balance your cup?

GUESS_____

TEST your Guess.

TELL_____

3. Empty the cups. Put your cup on the 4-inch mark on the ruler. Put 10 pennies in the taped-on cup. How many pennies must you put in your cup to balance the taped-on cup?

GUESS_____

TEST your Guess.

TELL_____

Seesaw Ups and Downs

III. Hee Haw, Seesaws

Experiment with your seesaw. How you can lift the most pennies or beans in your cup with the fewest in the taped-on cup?What did you discover?

_____

_____

_____

_____

_____

_____

_____

Ramp Romp

Team members: _____

_____

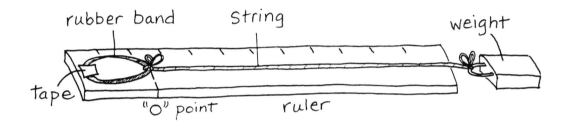

rubber band   string   weight

tape   "0" point   ruler

I. Make a Force Meter

1. Take a ruler and tape a rubber band to one end.

2. Tie a piece of string to the other end of the rubber band.

3. Lay the rubber band on the ruler. Straighten the rubber band out, but don't pull it. Mark "0" on the ruler next to the end of the rubber band.

4. Tie something heavy to the string.

What happens when you pull the object with the Force Meter?

_____

_____

Tie on a heavier object. Pull it with the Force Meter. Does anything change?

_____

_____

II. Ramp Romp

1. Build a ramp with your team. Use books and a flat, smooth surface like a board.

2. Measure your ramp.

How long is it?_____inches

How high is it?_____inches

3. Use your Force Meter to pull something heavy up the ramp. Ask your partner to mark how far the rubber band stretches on the ruler.

4. Now use the Force Meter to lift the object to the top of the ramp. Mark how far the rubber band stretches.

5. Which takes more force? **(circle one)**

        Lifting an object   Pulling it up a ramp

6. If you had a heavy load, would you lift it or pull it up a ramp? Why?

_____

_____

_____

_____

Weed Machines

shovel

rake

hoe

no tool

1. Which tool or tools did you use to weed? Circle the box showing the tool or tools. Circle the last box if you used your hands.

2. What was the best way to hold the tool for weeding? Draw arms and hands on the person in your box. Show how you held the tool or used your hands.

The Best Tool for the Job

1. If you wanted to weed again, which tool would you choose?

_____

2. Why would you choose this tool?

_____

_____

_____

3. What makes a good weeding tool work well?

_____

_____

_____

Invent a Tool

Inventors:_____Date_____

_____

1. Brainstorm about the garden tool you want to invent.

• What job needs to get done in the garden?

• How could a new tool help do the job easier?

• What kind of invention could solve the problem?

• What parts would I put together to make the invention?

Use the space below to draw your tool or write notes about it.

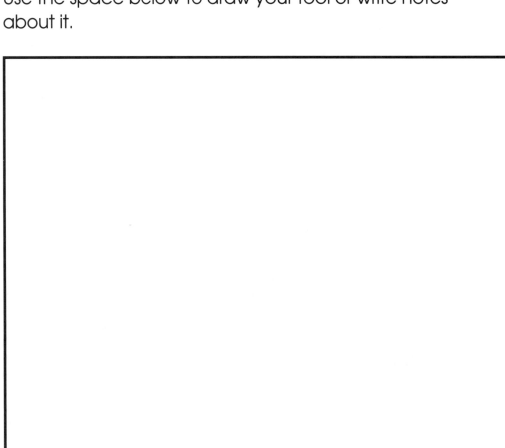

2. What will your tool do?

_____

_____

_____

3. What parts will it have?

_____

_____

_____

4. What materials will you need to make the tool?

_____

_____

_____

Postassessment

Name_____Date_____

The woodpecker! A woodpecker at work is like a hammer and chisel. The beak is the chisel. The woodpecker's tongue is barbed like a fish hook. It hooks insects and pulls them out of cracks in wood.

Write or draw some things you learned about tools and work. (Draw on another sheet of paper.)

_____

_____

_____

_____

Sea otters use tools. Otters eat shellfish. The shell is very hard. Otters use stones to crack open the shells. The otters float on their backs and place a stone on their chest. Then they pound the shell against the stone until the shell cracks open.

Questions I still have about tools and work:

_____

_____

_____

_____

Chimpanzees are tool-users. They use stones, leaves, and twigs for different things. Chimps love termites. They fish for them with a stick. Chimps push a stick into a termite nest. The termites attack the stick and hold on with their powerful jaws. The chimp pulls out the stick and eats the termites.

The Life Lab BEAT

FOCUS ON TOOLS

The Amazing Wooden Ox

Imagine a time with no airplanes, no trains, and no buses. You need to get food to people who are far away. You need to get the supplies through narrow mountain passes. What do you do?

Let's time travel to find out. Let's go back about 1,600 years. Now we're in China with a general named Chuko Liang. It was Chuko Liang who had to get food and supplies to his soldiers. Carts were too wide for the mountain passes. What did the general do? He invented the "wooden ox," or wheelbarrow!

The wheel on the general's wheelbarrow was much bigger than the wheel on your garden wheelbarrow. The wooden-ox wheel was about 4 feet across and had a dozen spokes.

The wooden ox was a huge success. In just a few years, people began building bigger and better wheelbarrows. Some carried people.

Now let's travel thousands of miles away to Europe. It's about 800 years ago. Imagine. There are no newspapers. No magazines. No TV. And no radio. We're with people who have never heard about the wooden ox in China.

These people have a problem to solve. They need to move heavy loads, too. They need to move dirt, crops, and other materials. How do they solve their problem? They invent a wheelbarrow too! Their wheelbarrow is not exactly like the Chinese wheelbarrow.

The Chinese wheelbarrow had one wheel in the center, right under the load. All the pusher had to do was steer and balance the cart. The European wheelbarrow had the wheel in front of the load. This meant that the pusher had to work harder. The wheel alone did not support the load. Today people use both kinds of wheelbarrow, depending on the kind of work they do.

Slinky—The Toy That Isn't a Toy

Nearly 50 years ago, an engineer named Richard James was testing different kinds of springs. He was trying to solve a problem. Ships are rocked by waves. The rocking affects navigation instruments. James wanted to invent a spring so that navigation instruments would not be affected by waves.

One day James accidently knocked one of his springs off a shelf. It "poured," coil by coil, onto a lower shelf. Then it dropped onto a stack of books. From there it moved to a table and finally came to rest on the floor. He was amazed. Then he placed it at the top of a flight of stairs and watched it drop step by step.

James had no idea what to do with his invention. Betty James, his wife, did. She saw it as a toy and even came up with a name—*Slinky*. The couple started a company to make and sell the toy. Children have been playing with Slinkys ever since.

During the war in Vietnam, soldiers tossed Slinkys over high tree branches to use as radio antennas. In the U.S., some farmers found a way to make Slinkys into a tool they use to pick pecans from trees.

Try It!

Play with a Slinky and see if you can come up with a new use for it. Can you find a way to use it in the garden? Around your house? At school?

How Things Work

Machines For Play

You use machines every day, even when you play on the playground. What kind of machine is a seesaw? A swing? A slide?

Do you play baseball? Did you know that when you hit the ball, your arm works as a lever and your muscles provide the force? Your elbow is the pivot.

How does the bat help you drive the ball farther? Think about it, then test your idea. Take a ball. Throw it in the air and hit it with your hand. Measure how far it goes. Then hit it with a bat. How far did it go this this time? Why? What made the difference? Does it matter how you hold the bat? Test it and see!

Folklore

Ideas from Nature

Where do great ideas for inventions come from? Many ideas have come from observing plants and animals. For example, over 200 years ago a French scientist got an idea from watching wasps. The wasps were chewing wood. They turned it to pulp with their saliva. Then they spread it on their nest. It hardened as it dried. What idea did the wasps give the scientist? The idea of making paper from wood.

Hundreds of years earlier, Chinese people watched silkworms spin their cocoons on mulberry trees. Someone figured out a way to unwind the cocoons and spin them into silken thread. Then people wove the thread into a shimmering cloth. The cloth they made is silk!

The Great Pyramid of Egypt

The Great Pyramid of Egypt is one of the wonders of the world. It was built over 5,000 years ago out of nearly 2 $\frac{1}{2}$ million stones. Each stone weighed anywhere from 5,000 pounds to 26,000 pounds. The stones came from quarries many miles away. The Egyptians had to drag them on sledges and then pull them up ramps to get them into place. Why didn't they use wheels? The wheel had not yet been invented.

It took 100,000 men over 20 years to build the pyramid. When they were finished, they had a building almost as tall as a modern skyscraper. It stands 480 feet high and covers 13 acres of land. It is not the largest pyramid in the world, though. The largest is in Cholulu de Rivadahia, Mexico. It is 177 feet tall and covers 25 acres. It was built around 2,000 years ago. And like the Egyptians, the builders had no wheels to help them. They, too, used ramps and levers.

Plants

Monday	Tuesday	Wednesday	Thursday	Friday

Month

Plants
Preassessment

Name_____Date_____

How many ways can you use roots?

What I know about the roots of plants:

_____

_____

_____

Can stems of trees take the heat?
Can you take a shower with a stem?

What I know about the stems of plants:

_____

_____

_____

How do leaves spice up your life?

What I know about leaves:

_____

_____

_____

_____

_____

Questions I have about plants and their parts:

_____

_____

_____

_____

_____

What's a Plant?

Name_____Date_____

1. Draw your plant and label its parts.

2. How is your plant like other plants?

_____

_____

_____

_____

_____

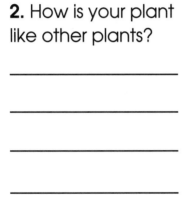

3. How is your plant different from other plants?

_____

4. What does your plant need to grow?

_____

_____

A Root View
Root View Record

Name_____Date_____

Draw the roots in the boxes below.

Week 1
How long are the roots?_____
How tall is the plant?_____

Notes_____

Week 2
How long are the roots?_____
How tall is the plant?_____

Notes_____

Week 3

How long are the roots?_____

How tall is the plant?_____

Notes_____

Week 4

How long are the roots?_____

How tall is the plant?_____

Notes_____

Dissect a Plant

Name _____ Date _____

Look at the drawing. Fill in the missing information based on your observations.

This plant part is a _____

I think it helps the plant because it: _____

This plant part is a _____

I think it helps the plant because it _____

This plant part is a _____

I think it helps the plant because it _____

Sun Blockers

Names_____Date_____

_____

GUESS: Why do leaves need light?

_____

_____

TEST: Color in each leaf to show what you did to it.

TEST

CONTROL

TELL: Color in your results.

TEST

CONTROL

Why do leaves need light?

_____

_____

Which Way is Up?

Names_____Date_____

_____

GUESS: How can we find out if roots always grow downward?

_____

What do you think will happen?_____

_____

TEST: Draw how the plants look now.   Date_____

Test   Control

TELL: Draw how the plants look now.   Date_____

Test   Control

What does this experiment show?

_____

_____

_____

_____

Why do you think this is so?

_____

_____

_____

_____

Rooting for Water

Names_____
_____

Date_____

Question: (What we want to know.)

_____

GUESS: (What we think will happen and why.)

_____

_____

TEST: (Describe the experiment.)

1. Our test: _____

2. Our control:_____

3. Steps we will take:_____

4. Use graph on back of this sheet for record keeping.

TELL: (What we observed.)

_____

_____

_____

Rooting for Water Graph

1. Each week measure the height of each plant. Measure the length of the roots, too.

2. Record the measurements by shading the number of centimeters. Write the date next to to the measurement.

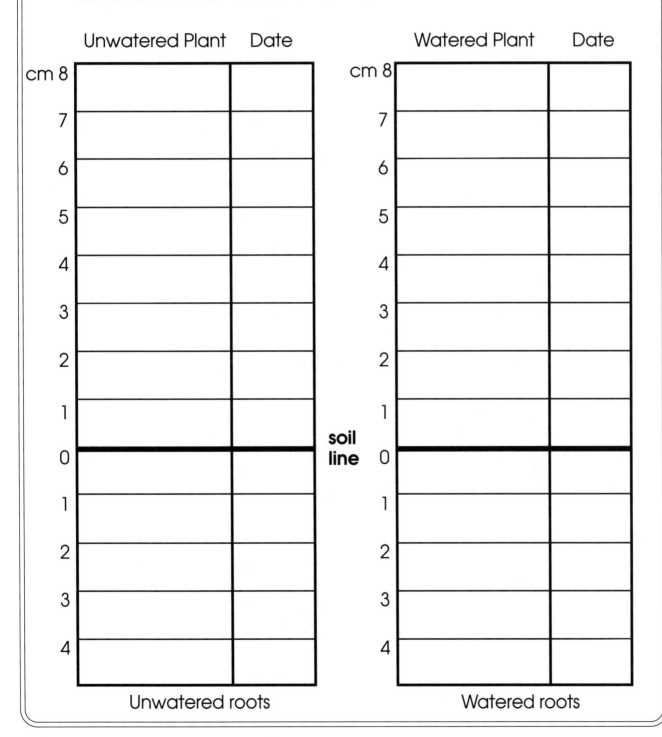

Amazing Plants

Names _____ Date _____

Question: _____

GUESS: (What do you think will happen and why.) _____

TEST: (Describe the experiment.)
Draw how you set up the maze and where you put the plant.

1. Our test: _____

2. Our control: _____

3. Steps we will take: _____
_____
_____

TELL: (What we observed.) _____

Draw how you set up the maze and where you put the plant.
Draw how the plant looks in the maze now. Date _____

Draw how the control plant looks.

How is the plant in the maze different from the control?

Why did the plant in the maze grow the way it did?

Get a Grip

Names_____Date_____

_____

Question: _____

_____

GUESS: (What do you think will happen and why.)

_____

_____

Test	Control

TEST: (Describe the experiment)

1. Our test: _____

2. Our control: _____

3. Steps we will take: _____

_____

TELL: (What we observed.)   Date_____

Test	Control

Why do some plants climb?

_____

_____

_____

_____

_____

Plant and Tell

Name_____

Date_____

Find an example of each of the
plants described below.

1. Find a plant bending to reach light.
How do you know? Where did you find it?

_____

_____

2. Find a plant that is twisting and climbing around
something else. How do you know? Where did you find it?

_____

_____

3. Find a plant that is not getting enough water. How do
you know? Where did you find it?

_____

_____

4. Find a plant that is not getting enough light. How do
you know? Where did you find it?

_____

_____

Postassessment

Name_____Date_____

Native Americans used plant roots to make food, clothing, baskets, and tools. Tamarack roots were used to sew together birch bark to make canoes. The huge taproot of a tamarack tree was used in colonial times to build ships.

What I Learned about Roots:

_____

_____

_____

_____

Questions I Still Have about Roots:

_____

_____

_____

_____

The stem of a tree is its trunk! The trunk of a
Giant Redwood is covered with thick bark.
The bark helps protect it from fire.

Sudsy material in the trunk of the Soaptree
Yucca was used for soap in the Southwest.

What I Learned about Stems: _____

_____

_____

Questions I Still Have about Stems: _____

_____

_____

For centuries, the leaves of herb plants have
been dried and used to season foods.

What I Learned about Leaves: _____

_____

Questions I Still Have about Leaves: _____

_____

The Life Lab

BEAT

FOCUS ON PLANTS

Life Lab Beat
Focus on Plants

Monkey Medicine

In the rainforests of Costa Rica, scientists watched howling monkeys. They watched as the monkeys sniffed and tasted leaves. Kenneth Glander was one of the scientists watching. He believes the monkeys were hunting for leaves to take as medicine.

The scientists also observed adult howling monkeys caring for their sick baby monkeys. The adults gave the sick babies certain roots and leaves. The researchers think the adults were teaching the young monkeys which plants would cure them.

Not only monkeys use plants as medicine. In Africa, scientists studying chimpanzees noticed something unusual. The chimps would sometimes eat leaves from a plant that wasn't part of their usual diet. This one plant is part of the sunflower family. Usually chimps grab a bunch of leaves and eat them. But when the chimps ate this plant, they did something different. They would take just one, and gulp it down whole. The chimps would wrinkle up their noses when they ate this bad-tasting leaf. Scientists are studying this plant to see if it is a source for human medicine as well.

Bears also seem to know something about medicine. According to Navajo legend, bears taught the tribe about a plant that can treat stomach aches and infections. Researchers decided to test the legend. They wanted to see if bears used this plant. They found that the bears do dig up the root mentioned in the legend. The bears chew the root and then rub it all over their bodies. There is something in the root that helps fight ticks.

It's not a surprise that plants are used as medicine. Humans already use medicine made from plants. For example, aspirin originally came from willow bark, and aloe vera juice is often used to help heal burns. But what is a surprise is that animals may be a new source of information about medicinal plants.

Salad Machine

We want fresh veggies! That's what astronauts say when they return from space. But there are no salad bars and no grocery stores in space. So what can the astronauts do about vegetables? Grow them!

Dr. Mark Kliss and other scientists at NASA Ames research center in California are developing ways for space travelers to have their fresh vegetables. Growing plants in space is a big challenge. It's not as easy as digging a garden bed. For one thing, dirt is a big problem, because the space station must be kept as clean as possible. Dirt turns to dust, it's messy—especially when mixed with water—and it's heavy! But if you can't grow plants in dirt, how can you grow them?

One way is by using hydroponics. That means growing plants in a mixture of water and nutrients. But water is a problem too. It has to be contained so it doesn't fly all over the space station.

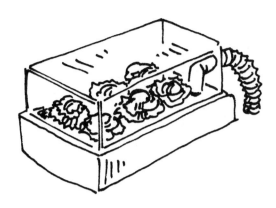

That's where the Salad Machine comes in. It's a kind of enclosed garden. It's not the perfect solution, but it is one that does work. The Salad Machine has about four enclosed trays kept in a refrigerator. The system provides the plants with the appropriate temperature, humidity, light levels, water, and nutrients they need to grow.

Not all plants grow well in the Salad Machine, but certain kinds of salad plants do—lettuce, radishes, Orbit carrots, and green onions, for example. Researchers also developed a special cherry tomato plant called Micro-Tom for use in the salad machine. The whole plant is only six inches high! The Salad Machine can provide a salad for a crew of four every other day.

What will the space travelers do with the roots, stems, and leaves that they don't eat in their salads? Bring them back to Earth where there is already a long list of scientists who want to study the effects of space travel on plants.

Root Candy?

Marshmallows were once made from the roots of a plant called the marshmallow. It grows along coasts and in marshes. Marshmallows are tall plants with soft, velvety leaves. Long ago, people dug up the roots of marshmallows. Then they boiled the roots until a thick syrup formed. People used the syrup to heal sore throats. It was very soothing. It also tasted good. Before long, someone added sugar to the syrup and let it thicken. They called the treat marshmallow candy. The marshmallows people buy today are no longer made from marshmallow roots, but the name remains.

Do Plants Communicate?

Bruce Mahall is a *botanist* (plant scientist) who claims that plants communicate with one another. He got the idea when he was working in the Mojave Desert in California. He was studying desert plants. Since there is very little water in the desert, he wondered whether the plants competed for water.

He observed that one kind of plant, the burro weed, interfered with the water supply of a nearby creosote bush, a different kind of plant. But burro weed did not interfere with the water supply of other burro weeds. He thought the roots might be communicating. He decided to test his idea.

First he built a box like a root view box. Then he grew the two different kinds of bushes. He observed the root growth every day to see how the roots behaved. He saw that the roots behaved in different ways. There seemed to be a type of root communication. The burro weed roots seemed to be able to tell when they were growing near another burro weed. When they detected another burro weed, they avoided it. By avoiding each other, the burro weeds did not compete with each other for the available water.

Bruce Mahall thinks there may be other kinds of root communication. He says scientists should pay more attention to what's going on underground.

Garden Animals

Name _____

Month _____

Monday	Tuesday	Wednesday	Thursday	Friday

Garden Animals
Preassessment

Name_____

Date_____

Why do ladybugs lay their eggs on plants covered with aphids?

What is the largest kind of insect?

What I know about garden animals:

_____

_____

_____

_____

_____

Questions I have about garden animals:

_____

_____

_____

_____

_____

How do male wolf spiders attract female spiders?

How can spiders fly?

What's in Our Garden?

Part 1

Name_____Date_____

Draw a quick sketch of the animal you have been following in the garden.

1. How can you tell this is an animal?

_____

_____

_____

_____

_____

2. Where did you find this animal?_____

_____

3. What did you watch this animal do?_____

_____

4. What do you think your animal needs to survive?_____

_____

What's in Our Garden?

Part 2

Name_____Date_____

Look at your animal carefully and draw it in the box below.
Be as accurate as you can.

1. What do you think this animal eats?

_____

_____

_____

2. Why do you think so?

_____

_____

_____

_____

3. How does this animal move?_____

_____

4. Why do you think so?_____

_____

5. What would you like to find out about this animal?_____

_____

6. What kind of animal is this? Look in animal identification books to tell.

_____

Finding, Watching and Drawing Wild Things

Watching Wild Things—
How to Hunt Using Only Your Eyes

1. Get down low. Pretend that you are the same size as your animal. Look under bushes and leaves.

2. Move only your eyes. Hold your body still. Let your eyes explore. Move slowly and quietly. Stop when your animal stops.

3. Listen. When you hear something move, look in that direction. Let your ears help your eyes.

4. Wear clothes that blend in with the garden. Wear soft shoes. Find or make something that will hide you.

How to Take Care of a Wild Thing

1. Set up a clear container with the things the animal needs.

If it lives in the soil, put in a layer of soil.

If it hides under rocks, put in a rock.

If it eats leaves, put in fresh leaves daily.

If it climbs twigs, put in a twig.

2. Poke small holes in the lid of the container so the animal can get fresh air.

3. Make sure the animal has water. Give it a bottle cap full of water, or a fresh slice of fruit or vegetable.

4. REMEMBER: the animal is only a guest. After a few days release it where you found it.

Tips for Finding Your Wild Thing

1. When is your animal busy? Some animals eat at night. Some eat in the morning.

2. Look in places where your animal can find food. Look in places where your animal might sleep.

REMEMBER: Leave the area the same way you found it!

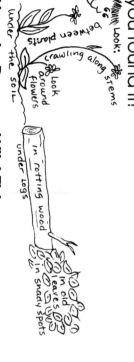

Look: between plants
crawling along stems
Look around flowers
under the soil
in rotting wood
under logs
in old leaves
in shady spots

How to Draw a Wild Thing

1. Start with a quick sketch. What is the animal's shape?

2. Draw the animal's feet. Where is it standing?

3. Quick! Draw its eyes! Draw its tongue! Draw its tail!

Keep going!

Tips for Catching a Wild Thing

You do not want to hurt your animal when you catch it. BE CAREFUL!

Does it fly?

Wait until it lands on a leaf or a twig. Then cover it with a jar or cup. When it flies up into the jar, cover the opening with a sheet of paper and set the jar down.

Does it crawl?

Lay a sheet of paper in the animal's path. When it crawls onto the paper, cover it with a clear jar.

Is it busy at night?

Put a jar down into the soil. Put some food in the jar. See if your animal falls into the trap.

open
Ground level
Dir t

Sense Abilities

Names_____Date_____

_____

The kind of animal we have is a_____.

1. Which body part do you use for each sense? Write or draw each of these parts in the ME column below.

2. Which of its body parts do you think your animal uses for each sense? Write or draw each of these parts in the MY ANIMAL column.

Where are the Senses?		
	ME	**MY ANIMAL**
See	_____	_____
Hear	_____	_____
Feel	_____	_____
Smell	_____	_____
Taste	_____	_____

Sense Abilities

The sense we will investigate is _____.

Write down some questions you have about how your animal uses this sense. Also include ideas of how to find out answers to your questions.

Question 1._____

_____

How we could test this question:_____

_____

Question 2._____

_____

How we could test this question: _____

_____

Question 3._____

_____

How we could test this question:_____

_____

Sense Abilities

GUESS
What we are going to find out about
our animal:

_____

_____

TEST
How we are going to find out:

Step 1: _____

_____

Step 2: _____

_____

Step 3: _____

_____

Step 4: _____

_____

Step 5: _____

_____

Approved by teacher _____

Sense Abilities

TELL
What happened?

First try: _____

_____

Any surprises?_____

_____

Second try: _____

_____

Any surprises?_____

_____

What does this tell you about your animal?_____

_____

_____

Animal Map

Team Members

Animal Keeper:_____

Timekeeper: _____

Place Keeper:_____

Animal Watcher:_____

1. The kind of animal we have:_____

2. Describe the motion your animal makes when it moves.

_____

3. Compare the speed of your animal to something else.

Our animal is as_____as a_____.
                        (fast, slow)

4. Draw a picture of the body parts your animal uses to move.

Animal Map

On the map below, mark where you put your animal's shelter and where you put its food.

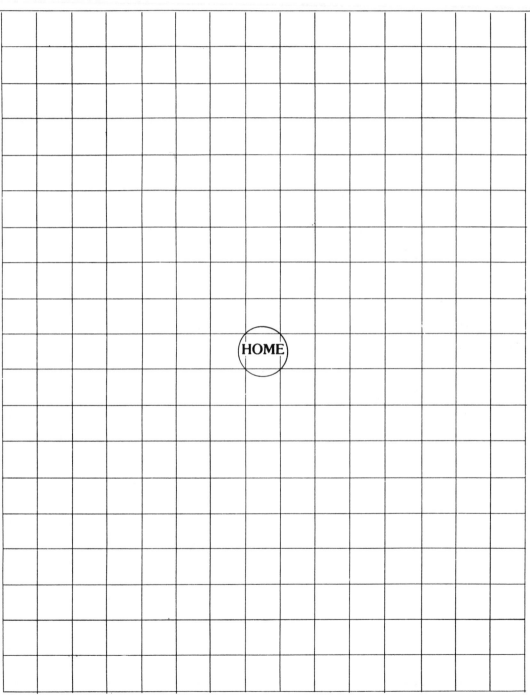

SCALE : ½ INCH = 1 MILE

Better to Eat You With

Name_____Date_____

1. Draw a line from the animal's mouthpart to the tool that is most like it.

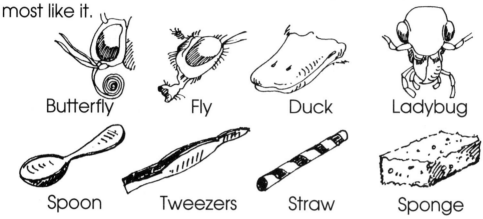

Butterfly   Fly   Duck   Ladybug

Spoon   Tweezers   Straw   Sponge

2. Draw a line from each animal to the food that it eats.

Nectar

Aphids

Wild rice and bread crumbs

Liquid

Better to Eat You With

Compare the tools in your group to find out which can carry the most of each substance. Put a 1 in that box. Put a 2 in the box of the tool that was next. Then give a 3 to the tool that followed, and a 4 to the tool that can carry the least amount of that food.

Feeding Tool Chart				
	Tweezers	Straw	Spoon	Sponge
Grain & Soil				
Water				
Floaters				

Safety First!

Name_____Date_____

Different animals react in different ways when they need to protect themselves. Some of the ways are listed below.

HIDE! An animal that cannot be seen is pretty safe. Some insects look just like leaves, thorns, or twigs. It is hard to tell they are even there! Others have colors that blend in with their surroundings. You might not see a grasshopper in the grass until it takes a high hop.

ATTACK! Some animals are able to fight back. A skunk sprays its enemy with stuff that stings and stinks! So does a skunk beetle. Ants have big biting jaws. Bees and wasps have stingers. Some toads can cover themselves with a substance that hurts your skin.

TRICK! Some insects act or look like something else. Flies that have the same coloring as bees are left alone. Monarch butterflies taste bad. Viceroy butterflies look like monarchs and birds pass them by just in case.

RUN! Some animals use their quick speed to get away from danger. They may run. They may fly. They may slither.

SCARE! Some animals are able to confuse their enemies and scare them away. Some caterpillars can swell up to look like snakes. The wings of some moths look like giant eyes.

PLAY DEAD! Some animals just stay put and hope that the enemy goes away. Some curl up into a tight ball. Safety First!

How do you think your animal defends itself?_____

_____

_____

Why do you think this?_____

_____

Draw a picture of your animal defending itself.

Sound Ideas

Name_____Date_____

Station 1: Sound Machine

1. Place the ruler so that the 1 and 2 centimeter marks are over the edge and the 3 centimeter mark is at the edge. Ask another student to hold down the part of the ruler on the table. Hold it down tightly!

2. Flick the part of the ruler that hangs over the table edge. What do you see?

_____

_____

What do you hear?_____

_____

3. Move the ruler so that the 20 centimeter mark is at the edge of the table. Flick the part of the ruler that hangs over the edge. Record your results on the chart on the next page.

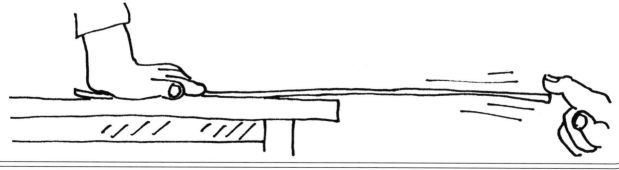

Sound Ideas

4. Do an experiment! Move the ruler to the 18 centimeter mark, and flick it. Now move it to the 15 centimeter mark, and flick. Next try the 12 centimeter mark. Record your data.

Sound Machine Data Chart		
Centimeter Mark	How fast does the ruler vibrate?	What do you hear?
20		
18		
15		
12		

At what centimeter mark did the ruler

vibrate fastest?_____Slowest?_____

At what centimeter mark was the

sound highest?_____Lowest?_____

When the ruler is vibrating fast, is the

sound high or low?_____Why?_____

_____

When the ruler is vibrating slowly, is the

sound high or low?_____Why?_____

_____

Sound Ideas

Station 2: Vibration Sensation

Step 1. If your drum is a coffee can with a plastic lid, go to Step 2. If not, follow these directions to make a drum. Stretch a piece of plastic or balloon over a can. Stretch it tight. Ask a classmate to put rubber bands around it to hold it down. If the drum skin is not tight enough, pull on the ends of the plastic or balloon piece.

Step 2. Sprinkle the top of the drum with the cereal, sand, salt, or popcorn.

Step 3. Roll a piece of construction paper into a megaphone. Now point the megaphone at the drum top, and SHOUT! (Do not blow through the megaphone. Shout!) Make your voice higher or lower, and shout again. Move the megaphone farther from the drum, and shout again.

Step 4. If you have a pan, hold it close to the drum. Beat on the pan with a ruler. Move the pan farther from the drum, then closer again. Try to make different sounds with the pan and ruler.

What happens when you shout or bang?_____

_____

What things vibrate when you shout or bang?_____

_____

Why do you think they vibrate?_____

_____

Sound Ideas

Station 3: String Strummer

1. Put a rubber band around your can, pan, or box. Strum the rubber band. What happens when you strum?

_____

_____

_____

2. Find a thicker, thinner, longer, or shorter rubber band. Stretch it next to the first one. Strum this rubber band. How is this rubber band different from the first?

_____

_____

How is its sound different from the sound of the first rubber band?

_____

_____

3. Put a pencil between one of the rubber bands and the tin or box. Twist the pencil to tighten the rubber band. Now strum the rubber band. What happens to the sound?

_____

_____

4. Put on some more rubber bands, and make a strummer. See if you can make each rubber band have a different sound.

_____

_____

Garden Animals
Postassessment

Name_____Date_____

Ladybugs lay their eggs on plants covered with aphids so when their young hatch from the eggs, they won't have to go far to find food.

Butterflies and moths are the largest kind of insects you will find.

What I learned about garden animals:

_____

_____

_____

_____

Questions I have about animals:

_____

_____

_____

_____

_____

A male wolf spider will dance and wave
his legs in front of a female in order to
attract her.

Ballooning spiders climb onto fence
posts or branches and release silk. As
the line gets longer the wind lifts the
spider and carries it off to a new area.

The Life Lab BEAT

FOCUS ON ANIMALS

An Ant's-Eye View

Did you know that there are more ants than any other creature on Earth? You'll find them everywhere. Ants live in the desert, on the seashore, on mountain slopes, and in the cracks of city sidewalks. They can survive in almost every climate on Earth.

Ants do not use their eyes to find their way. Instead they use a pair of long feelers called *antennae*. Antennae are used for feeling, smelling, picking up vibrations, and even taking temperatures. Ants even use their feelers to communicate. An ant carries a chemical in its jaw that signals an alarm. If you step on an ant, the alarm goes off and all the ant soldiers quickly appear, ready to go to war.

Ants are very smart. To test them, a group of scientists built a special ant maze. The ants had to find their way through the maze to reach a dish of food. Then they had to take the food back. The scientists found that once the ants had figured out the maze, they would quickly reach the dish the next time by following their own scent trail. Even when the scientists removed the scent trail, the ants still got through the maze. They had apparently memorized the right path.

Batty about Bats

What animal can fly in complete darkness through winding tunnels, miss hitting even tiny objects, and find insects almost too small to be seen? A bat! How does a bat do this? Over 200 years ago, Lazzaro Spallanzani of Italy and his partner, Louis Jurine of Switzerland, decided to find out. Here's what they did.

The two scientists experimented with a group of bats. They covered the ears of a number of bats, but not their eyes. The two men were surprised by what they discovered. The bats could see, but they kept bumping into large objects. They even bumped into each other! From the experiment, it seemed clear that the bats did not use sight to direct their flight. Instead they relied on sounds.

But if bats used their ears and not their eyes to find their way, what sounds did they hear? The two scientists could only hear the sound of the bats' wings. What could the bats hear?

The sound mystery stayed a mystery for over 100 years. Then, in 1920, an English scientist named H. Hartridge had an idea. He wondered if the bats used *ultrasonic* sound to find their way. Ultrasonic sound is too high a pitch for human ears to hear. Many animals, however, can hear ultrasonic sounds.

Hartridge tested his idea. He found that a bat makes squeaking noises that bounce off nearby objects. The echo from the object tells the bat how far away the object is. It also tells the object's size and shape. Using echoes, a bat can find and catch as many as 600 insects in an hour. Some of those insects are as thin as a hair. Yet the bat finds them even in total darkness.

The way a bat uses sound to see is called *echolocation*.

The Turtle Stomp

Zoologist (animal expert) John Kaufmann observed something unusual. He saw a wood turtle stomping eight times with one foot and then eight times with the other. He thought at first that the turtle was sick. Then he noticed that it was eating earthworms.

Dr. Kaufmann decided to try an experiment. He did the turtle stomp himself. He tapped two fingers on the ground just the way the turtles stomped their feet, and up popped earthworms.

Kaufmann thinks the worms came up because they believed the noise came from a mole tunneling in the ground. Moles eat earthworms. So the worms tried to escape, only to be eaten by the wood turtles.

How Things Work

The Hum of the Hummingbird

Do hummingbirds really hum? Not when they sing. The hummingbird song is a chirping sound. Their wings make the humming noise. They beat their wings backward and then forward in a figure eight shape from 50 to 90 times a second. This movement allows the bird to hover in mid-air above a flower, and then rise straight up like a helicopter.

You Can Judge a Bird by Its Beak

The beautiful pink flamingo has a curved beak with a downward hook. This bird is a *filter feeder*. Its beak is like a sieve. When it feeds, the flamingo wades into the water on its long legs, and lowers its neck so that its curved beak hangs up-side down. Then it swings its beak from side to side, filtering water for plants and small living creatures.

Birds that eat seeds have short, thick beaks that are good for cracking open shells. Birds that live in ponds have bills that are flat and broad. Why would they need a scoop-like beak? Birds of prey have powerful beaks with the upper beak hooked over the lower beak. The tree creeper uses its bill to find insects and spiders.

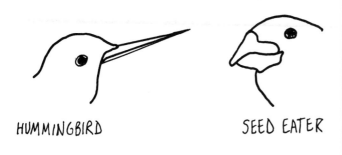

HUMMINGBIRD   SEED EATER

It's a Record!

Bird Records

Largest bird

The male African ostrich stands 2.5 meters (8 feet) tall and can weigh as much as 155 kilograms (340 pounds).

Smallest bird

The ee hummingbird of Cuba is 60 millimeters (2.25 inches) and weighs only about 2 grams (0.07 ounces).

Fastest flier

The spine-tailed swit flies at about 170 kilometers (106 miles) per hour.

Fastest diver

The duck hawk and the golden eagle can dive at speeds of up to 290 kilometers (180 miles) per hour.

Fastest runner

The ostrich can maintain a speed of 55 kilometers (35 miles) per hour, with bursts up to 80 kilometers (50 miles) per hour.

Animal Speed Records

Animal	Km/hr	MPH
cheetah	112	70
lion	80	50
gazelle	80	50
hare	72	45
race horse	64	40
shark	64	40
rabbit	56	35

A snail moves at about .05 kilometers (.03 miles) per hour. How fast can you run?

Habitats

Month

Name

Monday	Tuesday	Wednesday	Thursday	Friday

Preassessment

Name_____Date_____

What kind of animal can you find in every habitat in the world?

1. What I know about habitats:

_____

_____

_____

_____

_____

2. Questions I have about habitats:

_____

_____

_____

_____

_____

_____

Follow That Ant!

Animal Trackers:_____

_____

Date_____

1. What animal did you track? Write its name or draw what it looks like.

[ ]

2. Where did you find it?

_____

_____

3. Did you see your animal eat?_____
If so, what did it eat?

_____

_____

4. Did your animal stay more in sun or shade?

_____

5. Was its habitat cold or warm?_____

6. Was its habitat wet or dry?_____

7. What other animals did you see in your animal's habitat?

_____

_____

_____

_____

_____

_____

Digging In

Naturalists:_____

_____

Date:_____

Naturalist's Field Survey

Were you a Garden Naturalist or a

Weed Bed Naturalist?

Circle one.

Keep notes on this survey sheet as you work.

Time of day:_____

Plot Number:_____

Number of animals I counted:_____

Number of plants I counted:_____

How many different kinds of animals did you find?

_____

Name the ones you know:_____

_____

How many different kinds of plants did you find?_____

Name the ones you know:

_____

_____

_____

What plant and animal names did you learn today?

_____

_____

_____

Glass Houses

Name_____Date_____

1. Draw a picture of how you want the terrarium to look.
Title the picture with the name of the habitat.

My Terrarium

_____ **Habitat**

2. As you create your terrarium, record information below about the parts of the habitat.

Kind of soil: _____

Climate: _____

Plants: Animals:

_____   _____

_____   _____

_____   _____

_____   _____

_____   _____

_____   _____

_____   _____

3. How will you take care of the terrarium?

_____

_____

_____

4. Describe the terrarium habitat you created, or draw a picture of it on another sheet of paper.

_____

_____

_____

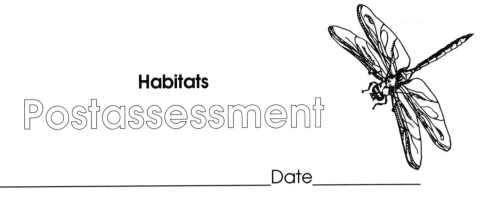

Postassessment

Name_____Date_____

Insects. You can find them in water, in forests, in deserts, on mountain tops. They are everywhere!

1. What I learned about habitats:

_____

_____

_____

_____

_____

2. Questions I still have about habitats:

_____

_____

_____

_____

_____

Vanishing Habitats

Tropical rainforests are disappearing. About 12 hectares (30 acres) are destroyed each minute. Does it matter? It matters a lot!

About half of all the plants and animals on Earth make their home in the rainforest. If they lose their home, they are in danger of becoming extinct. That means they disappear forever.

A rainforest is one kind of habitat. It is a woodland that gets about 60 inches of rain each year. Most rainforests are near the equator.

Scientists divide a rainforest into layers—like the stories in an apartment building. Each layer is home to many plants and animals. The top layer is called the *canopy*. Here the treetops get lots of sunlight and rain. The middle layer, called the *understory*, is darker. Creepers and

climbing plants grow here. So do young trees struggling to reach the light. The next layer is even darker. It is called the *herb layer*. It is where shrubs and very young trees grow. Very little sunlight can reach the *ground layer*. It is the darkest of all. It is also very damp.

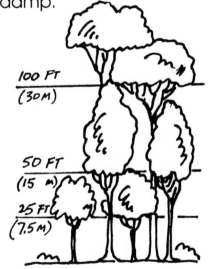

100 FT
(30M)

50 FT
(15 M)

25 FT
(7.5 M)

The plants and animals who live in each layer in the rainforest depend on one another. As leaves and fruit from the tall trees decay and fall, they provide food for animals. They also enrich the soil and keep it fertile. Without the trees, the heavy rains would wash away nutrients in the soil. Then when the rain stopped, the hot sun would bake the soil so that plants could not grow.

Rainforest plants are very important. Many medicines are made from plants that grow in the rainforest. The plants also help keep the Earth's air clean. They take carbon dioxide from the air and put oxygen into it. About 40 percent of the world's oxygen comes from the forests.

But not just rainforests are in trouble. Other habitats are vanishing, too. Many people all over the world are working hard to save habitats before it's too late.

Scientists at Work

Garden Pals

It's a jungle out there! Look around you. Everywhere there are bugs attacking other bugs, bugs attacking plants, plants attracting bugs. It's endless.

For some scientists, like Francisco Rosado-May, the jungle is a living laboratory. Rosado-May thinks that we can learn a lot by observing what goes on in that jungle. Rosado-May is an *agroecologist* working in Mexico. He is studying the ways that insects and plants interact in nature. He is very interested in finding ways of controlling pests the way nature does.

Why study in Mexico? In Mexico farmers have been farming *milpas*, or fields, for thousands of years. They don't use any pesticides and they grow lots of different crops together, such as corn, beans, and squash. Rosado-May wants to learn how the farmers can grow so much food in a small area and not need pesticides.

Some plants attract insects that protect the plants. One day, while working in a milpa, Rosado-May found a sick-looking caterpillar. He took it back to his lab to observe it.

A few days later the caterpillar died. Francisco cut it open and found eggs. He remembered that he had read about a wasp that lays her eggs inside caterpillars. The caterpillars get sick and die. Francisco wondered if the eggs he found were wasp eggs. He watched the eggs, and soon wasps hatched out! He discovered that these wasps help protect the corn from the leaf-eating caterpillars.

But it's not the corn that attracts the wasps. It's the bean plants that do. Wasps use bean-flower nectar as food. The female wasp lays her eggs inside caterpillars that are on corn plants. If the farmers only grew corn, the wasps wouldn't be there.

Francisco Rosado-May plans to keep looking in the milpas for other ways that plants and animals work together.

How Things Work

Saving a Habitat

"You can make a difference." That's what the members of the Children's Ecology Club in San Diego, California, think. And they should know. They are making a difference. They just helped save 2.2 acres of land that is the habitat of an endangered plant.

The project started in 1990 when students at Joe Hickman Elementary School decided to adopt an endangered species. The students adopted a plant called the San Diego mesa mint. The plant lives in the middle of a development area, and was in danger of being destroyed by people tromping on it, and by tree roots crowding it. Club members met at the site, identified the plant, and decided to try to save the mesa mint. With the help of their advisor, Dr. Kathryn Wild, club members circulated petitions, hung posters, and got their message out. This particular site is now protected, but the club members are not stopping there.

The club is growing. Members have plans to adopt another local, endangered plant species. San Diego button-celery is next on their list.

If you live in California and are interested in adopting a California endangered species, contact:

National Audubon Society
Richardson Bay Center
376 Greenwood Beach Rd.
Tiburon, CA 94920

If you live in another state and are interested in an adoption program, contact one of the following organizations:

The International Crane Foundation
E-11376 Shady Lane Rd.
Baraboo, WI 53913-9778

Save the Manatee Club
1101 Audubon Way
Maitland, FL 32751

Whale Adoption Project
320 Gifford St.
Falmouth, MA 02540

Plant a Tree!

In 1872, Julius Sterling Morton was governor of Nebraska. He wanted to replace the trees that the settlers had cut down when they built farms, houses, and roads. So he offered prizes to the county that planted the most trees. That first year, over one million trees were planted in Nebraska!

Today people there have a special holiday to honor trees. It is called Arbor Day. In Nebraska, it is celebrated on April 22, Governor Morton's birthday. In other states, people observe the holiday on other days, usually in March or April. Find out when Arbor Day is in your state. And plant a tree.

TO UNDEVELOPED PLACE

My Journal

190